LIVING

in small spaces

LIVING
in small spaces

LOFT

Editorial coordination:
Cristina Paredes

Editor:
Cristian Campos

Translation:
Martin Douch, Bridget Vranckx

Art director:
Mireia Casanovas Soley

Layout:
Anabel Naranjo

Editorial project:
©LOFT Publications
Via Laietana, 32 4.º of. 92
08003 Barcelona, España
Tel.: 0034 932 688 088
Fax: 0034 932 687 073
e-mail: loft@loftpublications.com
www.loftpublications.com

ISBN: 978-84-95832-83-2

Printed in China

Index

Introduction

Does a painting need an immense canvas to be considered a master-piece? Leonardo da Vinci's "Mona Lisa" is 30 inches high by just over 20 inches wide. "Van Gogh's room in Arles" is 22 inches high by 29 inches wide. The obvious, instinctive answer is that there is no relationship what-soever between the size of the canvas and the originality of a work of art, even if the latter could be measured. But does the same apply to interior design? Can one deliver a creative, balanced, elegant and comfortable inte-rior design in a small apartment of 300 to 400 square feet? This book shows that it is indeed possible.

The progressive shrinking of city apartments, together with the wide-spread increasing cost of housing, has led to a search for interior designs that make the most of the area available, natural light sources and storage space. Hence the success of multinationals such as Ikea, who have made a virtue of necessity by thinking up a decorative "ideology" based on the idea of taking full advantage of the space and designing furniture that has been devised and manufactured to be used in much reduced and constant-ly changing spaces. Interior designers and decorators have also had to adapt quickly to this new reality by implementing resources and devices that are hardly ever used in larger homes. The result is a philosophy of life centered on the small-scale, the flexible and the adaptable. It is not only the size of the apartments that has changed; our style of life has also been altered along with it.

The projects included in this book have been chosen for their originality, their creativity (at times enormous) and their ability to take full advantage of the most awkward of spaces, with "awkward" here being a synonym for "lack of space". The intelligent use of colors, the exploitation of redundant corners, the popularization of multi-purpose shelving and materials that are more modern, lighter and visually trendier than traditional ones all help to turn a tiny industrial-style loft into a comfortable, functional living space. Spectacular advances in the field of industrial design also encourage exper-imenting with new forms and styles for furniture, which is constantly being adapted to new requirements.

Devised as a visual guide to show solutions applied by architects and inte-rior designers in small spaces, Living in Small Spaces is also an essential reference for all those who wish to discover the latest advances in interior design and decoration. Because, in fact, never has so much been done with so little. Or rather, in such a small space.

House in Barcelona

In this small apartment in Barcelona, the choice has been to maximize the little space available by means of a set of sliding panels that can be moved all round the edge of the home thanks to some rails set in the ceiling. The panels act as a decorative feature – dozens of holes have been made in them which fleck the whole surface – but also as a structural component: screens which help to redistribute the spaces as the owners wish. The adaptable furniture means that one space can quickly be changed into another one that is completely different: the square table in front of the sofa turns into a bedside table, while the sofa becomes a double bed, just three feet from the kitchen which at night is hidden behind the sliding panels. The result is an apartment that is functional and practical, adaptable and flexible, in which the lack of space is no obstacle to acquiring the maximum of comfort.

Mobile panels are an original and useful way of organizing the spaces of this small apartment.

The kitchen occupies one of the four walls
in the apartment, and its striking orange
color separates it visually from the rest
of the spaces in the house.

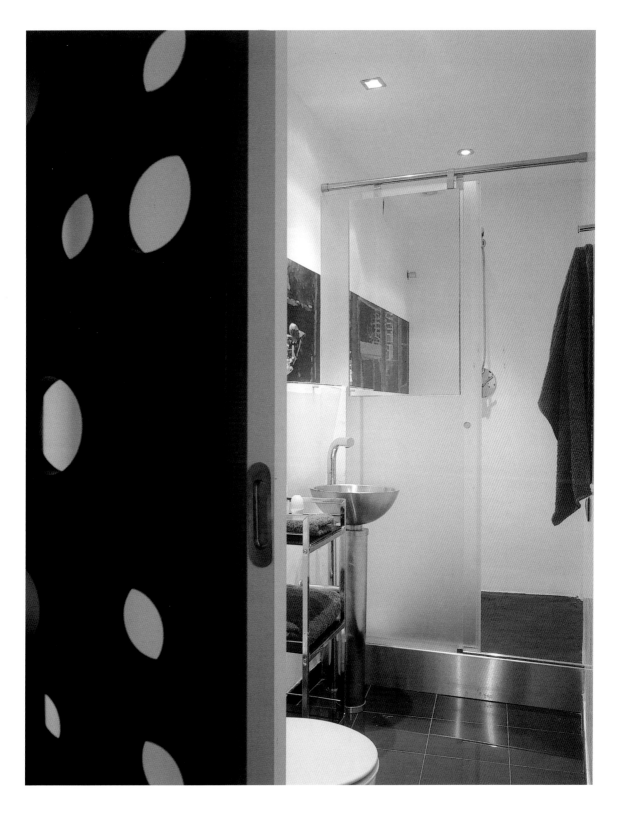

Apartment in West Village

This very small New York apartment has been carefully planned and structured to make the most of the space available. To achieve this, a stainless steel platform has been built coming out from halfway up the back wall of the apartment. A relaxation area has been installed on this platform (not the bedroom, which is on the lower floor) and underneath it, the kitchen. A lighting system installed on the structure lights both spaces evenly.

The three utility spaces (kitchen, bathroom and laundry) have been put all along the back wall to make the most of the space and to enable the rest of the apartment to be as open-plan as possible. In addition, the outside wall of the bathroom, of etched glass, takes advantage of the natural light.

The kitchen's work area separates this space from the dining room, though still allows communication with the rest of the room.

The space over the kitchen, which is small and more like an attic than a conventional room, benefits from the considerable height of the apartment's ceilings.

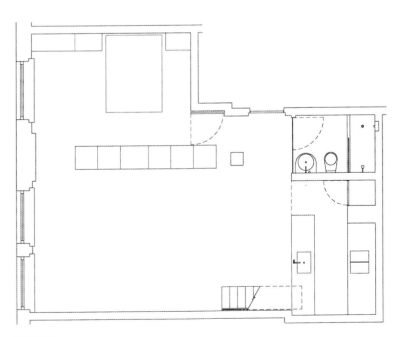

Floor plan

Araceli Manzano, Esther Flavià | Barcelona, Spain

Photos: © Eugeni Pons

Home in Barcelona

This small Barcelona apartment is an example of how to take a small space and exploit it to the maximum. To distinguish the various zones of the apartment, the designers have made clever use of colors: blue for the kitchen, yellow for the work area and bathroom, cream for the bedroom and white for the dining area. The result is an apartment that is cheerful, sparkling and structured extremely rationally, with a predominance of straight lines on the shelving, the tables – such as the work desk – the bench for the dining table and the panels separating the various spaces.

The parquet flooring provides the apartment with warmth, while the pop-art-inspired curved chairs contrast with the straight-edged shapes surrounding them. Clever use of fabrics, rugs and upholstery give the apartment a youthful and bold atmosphere.

A conscious design helps integrated the small kitchen in the center of the apartment into the rest of the home.

The double bed has been installed on a wooden platform that defines the sleeping area and separates it visually from the rest of the spaces in the house.

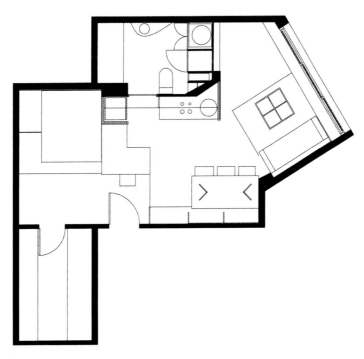

Floor plan

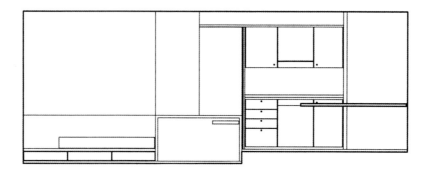

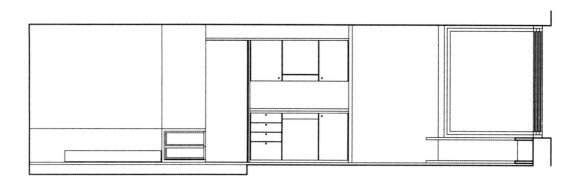

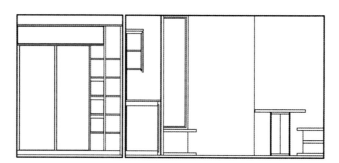

Sections

Apartment in Dornbirn

This small apartment in the town of Dornbirn sports some of the tried and trusted solutions for exploiting space: reducing circulation areas to the minimum; the use of natural or light-looking materials – such as wood or glass – and the elimination of interior dividing walls. The growing popularity of lofts in recent years is due more to the lack of space, an increasing problem in large urban agglomerations, than to the owners' choice, although one can of course find lofts of over 1,000 ft^2. Here it has been decided to do away with all surplus elements and reduce the furnishings down to three basic pieces: the bed, a wooden work-top that contains the hob and also does duty as a dining table, and a closet that acts as a separator, behind which a tub has been placed in the manner of a bath. The gabled roof is the main aesthetic interest of the apartment.

The right choice of furniture makes sure that the space beneath the slanting roof does not seem smaller.

The mixture of apparently heterogeneous decorative features, such as the wooden bench covered in cowhide, the rustically-inspired chairs and the ornamental feature imitating a reindeer's head give the space an avant-garde air.

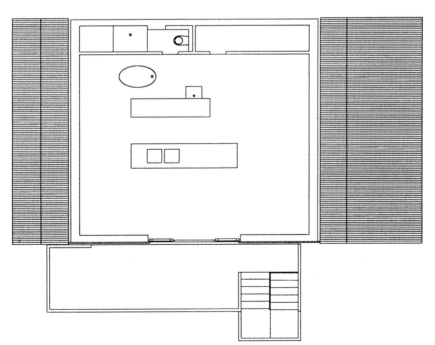

Floor plan

Flat in Lisbon

The elongated shape of this small apartment, similar to a fairly wide passage, made it extremely difficult to divide the space into rooms and make the best use of it. The solution lay in installing groups of modular shelving occupying practically the whole length of one of the apartment's two walls. The modules take on the form of a comb, and "coat" the dividers between the various areas of the house. The shelves in these modules serve mainly as storage space, although they have also been used to hold various decorative features. The result is an eminently functional apartment where the most has been made of all possible storage possibilities without sacrificing warmth. The fact that the home has natural light, leaving only the two central spaces reliant on artificial lighting, helps to give it a transparent, open atmosphere.

The austerity of the limited and functional furniture is one of the elements that characterize the decoration of the apartment.

The light parquet flooring and the white
of the walls and shelves helps to make
the most of the natural light coming in
through the windows of the main area
of the house, the living room.

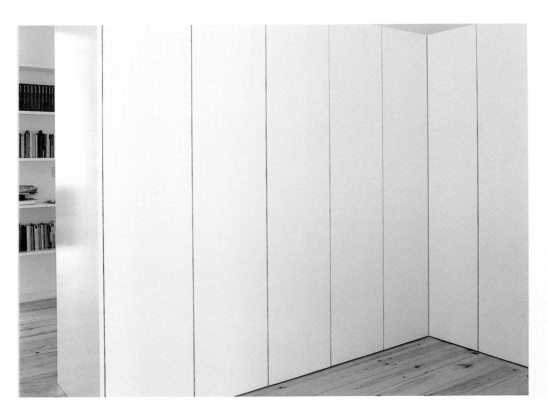

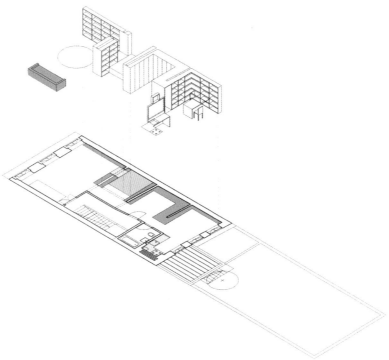

Exploded axonometry

House in Chelsea

In this apartment, one of the priorities has been to make the most of the natural light. To achieve this, an 18-inch gap has been left between the partition separating the bedroom from the rest of the apartment and the wall supporting the work table. This means that the light coming in through the bedroom window reaches the middle of the living room. Furthermore, the living room wall unit, three feet high, enables the light coming in through the window opposite to reach the mirrors on the back wall, which in turn distribute it to all corners of the room. The basically square shape of the apartment lends itself to these types of solution.

Each one of the spaces, such as the study or the kitchen, is excellently organized in the apartment's floor plan.

The space-saving built-in closets avoid the
proliferation of shelves and other storage
furniture.

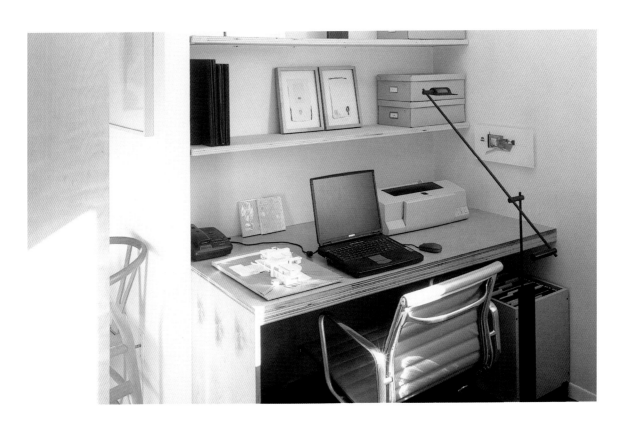

Floor plan

Small home in Berlin

Intensive building and rapid population growth in cities such as Berlin explain the progressive downsizing of homes. This means that very few people are privileged to have a patio like the one in this apartment, owned by the architects Jean-Marc Abcarius and Christopher Burns. The front of the apartment looks onto the street; at the back, there is an interior patio that has been turned into a small urban oasis. The apartment, with a ground plan that is almost square, has been laid out so that the owners' bedroom and the living room are at the front of the home, while the kitchen is masked between two partitions. The apartment has essentially been designed as an open space in which only the bedroom and bathroom are separated from the rest of the rooms by walls.

The patio can be reached from two different places: from the bedroom and from the dining room.

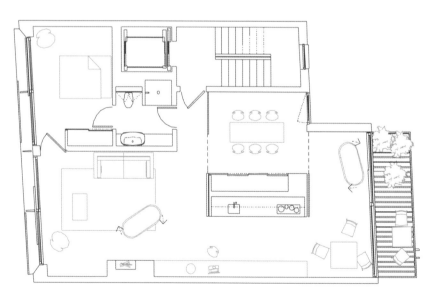

Floor plan

The large windows at the front and rear of the apartment, and the almost total absence of structural obstacles separating the various spaces enable the light to penetrate the apartment from front to back.

Home in Stockholm

The refurbishment of this 19th-century apartment in Stockholm, measuring barely 700 ft^2, centered mainly on the bedroom, kitchen and bathroom, with a markedly Scandinavian look, in which light-colored timber, pure straight lines and the colors white, cream, and ochre predominate. The only exception is the kitchen, whose green color partially breaks with the almost Zen-like atmosphere of the rest of the apartment. The kitchen and bathroom are on either side of the same partition, while the apartments' central space is divided into two clearly distinct rooms: first, the living room and then, the bedroom and dining area, separated by the partition against which the double bed and bedside table rest. The layout of the two main rooms means that the whole house, except for the entrance passage, has plenty of natural light.

Due to the apartment's small dimensions, it was necessary to carefully study the best location for each room.

Light colors, such as white and cream, and softer shades of yellow are the most appropriate for walls, soft furnishings and lamps in order to make the most of natural light.

Sections

Urban Living 1

The Urban Living 1 project, begun in 1997 and completed in 2001, is to be found in a densely populated area of Berlin. The front of the building breaks with the traditional separation of public and private space, typical of Central European countries, by means of a set of glass panels that opens it up fully to the exterior. In order to fine tune this extroversion, sliding panels have been built inside all the apartments in the building, enabling the owners to redistribute the spaces and hide them from the neighbors' eyes. The architects have interpreted privacy as an open, non-absolute concept, which can be varied depending on how keen one is to be seen from the outside. The fusion of the various spaces in the apartment – kitchen, living room, bedroom – changes the conventional perception of these rooms and gives them a relaxed, Mediterranean atmosphere: owners feel they are showering in the bedroom, cooking in the living room or relaxing in the kitchen.

The kitchen worktop can be extended and has multiple uses: it can be turned into a dining room or office.

Here we can see one of the sliding glass panels that can change the layout of the various spaces in the home, increasing or reducing them to suit the owner.

Slender Bender

Designed as a dual-purpose building – containing homes as well as offices – Slender Bender acts as an urban link between the university buildings in south Berlin and the ring of housing blocks in the north of the city. Despite its eminently futuristic appearance, the building, with a ground area of 5,400 ft2, blends in perfectly with its surroundings without disturbing the traditional activity and look of the area it is situated in. The apartments and the offices in the building are completely open to the exterior through windows that let in natural light. The first four floors of the building have been specially designed to be divided into two different studios or kept as just one area. The top two floors form a single space of interconnected offices.

The decoration of each studio can easily be personalized thanks to the brightness and simplicity of the spaces.

Photos: © Carlos Domínguez

Apartment by Ben Haitsma

Dozens of little interior design ploys aimed at saving space and making the most of natural light have turned this small London apartment into a space that is comfortable, full of light and entirely practical. The proliferation of points of artificial light, the white of the walls, the clever use of corners and unusable spaces, especially in rooms with an attic wall, and the small cupboards over the head of the double bed are just some of these ploys. The use of furniture made with materials that look light, such as plastic, glass or aluminum, also helps to give the home lightness and expression. The darkwood parquet, however, tones down this effect and provides warmth to the apartment, creating an interesting contrast between the two environments.

All the necessary elements in the kitchen are placed in a practical way, thus making the most of the available space.

The work table has been placed in the gap
between one of the interior bedroom walls
and the exterior attic wall of the home.

Frankie Loft

An attic has been built on this small apartment in Barcelona which gives it a second floor, used by the owners as a bedroom. The fact that the attic is supported on one of its sides by a light metal column (instead of on partitions) means that the lower floor, where the living room and kitchen are, is open-plan, with hardly any structural element to block the light coming in through the windows, lighting up all corners of the apartment. The use of violet and red in most of the furniture and decorative details gives conceptual unity to the space and provides it with a powerful individuality. The walls, of bare brick painted white, and the ceilings, where the old timber beams have been preserved, are further attractive features.

Despite the apartment's reduced dimensions, the ceiling's height increases the feeling of spaciousness.

The contrast between the metallic color of the ornamental beam, the white of the walls and the ceiling beams, on the one hand, and the red of the soft furnishings, the bedside table and the cushion, on the other, endow the home with individuality.

78 | Joan Bach

Fasan Home

In many cases, minimalism represents a reaction to chaos, massification and the aggression on the senses by the thousands of visual stimuli in large contemporary cities. In this respect, this apartment in Vienna is an example of how minimalism may be implemented in a small space without the result lacking in individuality and strength. In this home, the smallest detail, including the bathroom fittings, has been designed to fit in with the original plan. Superfluous elements have been eliminated and irregularly-shaped doorways have been opened up to break the visual monotony that is usually associated with minimalist interiors. The clever contrast of materials – timber, stainless steel and glass – and an elegant use of colors and their most appropriate combinations are further attractions in this apartment.

The risky, yet successful distribution of this home can be described as contemporary and original.

The living room is an open space at the end of which the work zone is hidden behind a glass panel. At the other end is an unusual built-in plant stand whose base hides a system of lights that light up the surface around it.

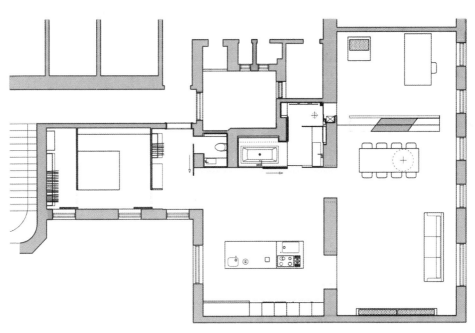

Floor plan

Loft in São Paulo

Keeping the iron beams and columns of the original structure, chipping at the walls to reveal the original brickwork
and forcing the contrast between the new and the old were
the three decisions taken by the architect, Brunete Frac-
caroli, when the Brazilian film director, Bruno Barreto, who
lives in New York, commissioned her to build this loft in São
Paulo. The result is an open-plan, functional space, brim-
ming with color and post-modern in its design, with the out-
standing feature being a glass attic that gives the apartment
a second floor without spoiling the visual aspect. The use of
glass panels as decorative elements fills the apartment with
color without removing any of its brightness. For the furnishings of the lower floor, however, moderation is the defining
element, perhaps to avoid upstaging these self-same colored glass panels.

By making the most of the height
of the ceiling, the loft acquires
surface area and the resulting
spaces are larger.

The motifs, a nod to the cinema, such as movie stills and reels, as well as a collection of cameras, turn this space into a small movie museum.

House in Melbourne

While it is impossible to increase the floor area of our home, we can exploit its spaces to the maximum to make the most of the last square foot. In this two-story home, situated in Melbourne, the utility areas (bathroom and kitchen, either side of one wall) have been joined together, and have been separated from the bedroom by means of a slate-colored cupboard which doubles as a partition, helping to mask the joining of the different types of flooring used in each of the three areas. This difference also helps to make a visual distinction between the three rooms. Access to the bathroom is from the bedroom, through the gap between the cupboard and the wall, and also from the kitchen.

Superfluous objects, which could overload the limited space of the apartment, were deliberately avoided in the furniture and decoration.

Dark-colored floors or those of rustic
materials are only advisable if the
apartment enjoys plenty of natural light.

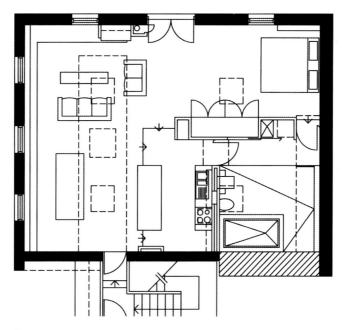

Floor plan

Sempacher Apartments

Situated in a residential neighborhood near the center of Zurich, the Sempacher Apartments are an example of architectural flexibility and adaptation to the surroundings. Although the project originally involved the restoration of the building that had occupied the site since 1930, it was finally decided to build a brand new block of apartments, which enabled the cost to be reduced considerably. The aim was to produce a pleasant, visually fluid building which would easily adapt to any changes, seamlessly blend in with the surrounding buildings, and whose appearance would take into account the life cycle of the materials used.

The bathroom and kitchen in the center of each apartment act as natural dividers of the space. The external wall of the bathrooms is of translucent glass, which enables the light to come inside.

The interior design follows the same lines as the design, fluidity and luminosity of the building.

The use of natural materials, such as timber, reinforces this integration of the apartments into their surroundings. The building is surrounded by a small park with grass, which keeps it apart from neighboring buildings.

Pied-à-terre in Miami Beach

This apartment in Miami answers the problems posed by its reduced size with a reasoned, logical layout. The kitchen is behind the only master wall in the apartment, and is separated from the relaxation area. On the other side of the wall is the shower, separated from the bathroom by a partition that is barely 6 feet long. The lavatory and hand basin have been installed in the bathroom. The stark decoration, almost obligatory given the reduced size, paradoxically provides a large room that doubles as a living room and dining room. The apartment has natural light coming in from the windows at either end, with a through draught, as well as a small patio with a wooden bench built against the exterior wall and handrail. The cheerful turquoise of the patio gives the home a beach atmosphere and integrates it into the surroundings, a garden with palm trees just a few yards from the shore.

The furniture helps create different areas, despite the smallness of the space.

The combination of different styles and designs in the furniture gives a cheerful, carefree identity to this apartment with white walls and industrial-style flooring.

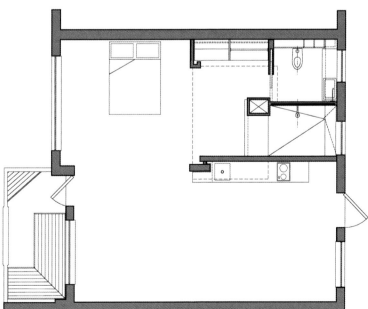

Floor plan

Loft in Bergamo

A cement staircase and a metal handrail whose banisters have been replaced with tautened metal cables are the central feature connecting the three levels of this apartment. On the lowest level is the bedroom; on the second, similar to an attic, is the living room which overlooks the bedroom, where a line of books doubles as a balustrade; on the upper level are the dining room and kitchen, made up of independent features that can be redistributed and easily moved to the owner's requirements. During the refurbishment of the apartment, the original wooden beams on the ceiling of the first and second floors were kept, and all potential natural light sources were exploited. The result is a home which, despite being divided into three small separate spaces, is uncluttered and very well lit.

The dining room is a small and cozy space, even though it only contains a television and a sofa.

The cross-beam rests on a wooden column which has also been painted white and also serves as support for the joists that support the ceiling of this room and the floor of the upper story.

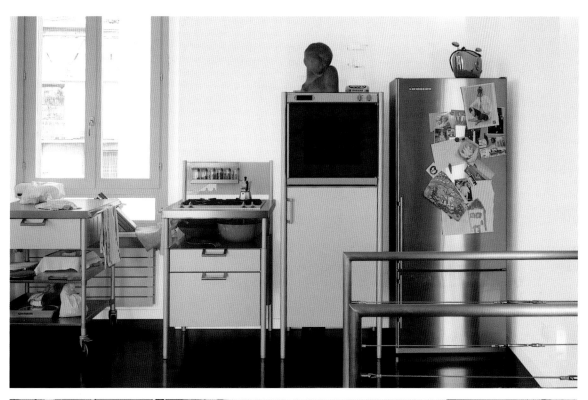

Apartment in Surry Hills

Situated in one of Sydney's fashionable neighborhoods, Surry Hills – a former working-class suburb packed with warehouses near the city center – this two-story studio has an upper floor consisting of the living room, dining room and kitchen, without any type of partition, and a lower floor containing the work area and the bathroom. Here we find a small shower room. On the lower level, the wooden joists supporting the floor of the upper level are exposed and rest on a large iron central beam crossing the apartment from end to end. On the upper floor, the gabled roof that covers it has been visually lowered by means of a set of wooden joists which also hold a bar with built-in spotlights lighting up the whole space equally. The dark-toned furnishings and a series of artificial light beams giving off a soft light endow the space with individuality.

The stone walls of the lower level and the modern furniture give the home character and personality.

The bright red of the carpet, the dark shades of the sofa and the dining table, the warm light from the wall lamps, the ceiling spotlights and the floor lamp provide an interesting visual contrast.

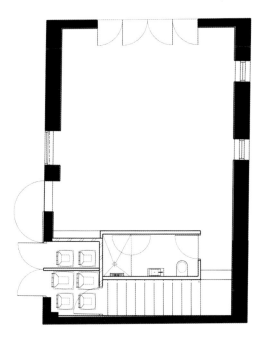

Ground floor

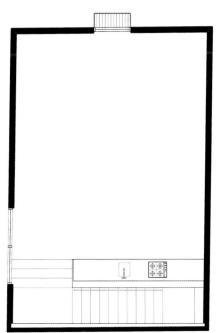

First floor

Home in Islington

The unique aspect of this apartment lies in the small decorative details and how these serve not just an aesthetic purpose but are also aimed at making rational use of the small space available. In the kitchen and bathroom, for example, all the elements have been chosen to occupy as little space as possible without looking out of place with the rest of the fittings. A wooden panel masking the WC cistern and the plumbing provides warmth to the room and eliminates the cold atmosphere that is typical of certain contemporary bathrooms. A rational distribution of storage space, such as the built-in closets and the small cupboards above the bed head, also helps to save extremely valuable space. The use of mirrors and materials such as glass or aluminum brightens up the apartment. Good natural and artificial lighting complete an interior design project that stands out for its effectiveness and practical results.

A contemporary and balanced space is created thanks to the choice of furniture and touches of color applied to the decoration.

The built-in closets are space-saving, and more so with an accordion door which folds in on itself rather than opening outwards.

Studio in Madrid

This studio in Madrid, with an area of 290 ft^2, has managed to grab a further 95 ft^2 thanks to its 11.5 feet of height. In this loft, reached by a wooden staircase with irregular steps, and built on a medium-density wood structure, there is a mattress, a sofa, a small cupboard and some shelves. On the lower level is a small compact kitchen, the dining table and a sofa surrounded by large cushions. Behind the stairs there is a cupboard just under 5 feet high and 6.5 feet deep that moves on castors, as well as the refrigerator and two other closets, used for storing clothes and situated in the entrance passage. The space left just above this storage area is 6.5 high, thus enabling easy access to the bedroom without the need to duck. Meanwhile, the kitchen is masked by folding doors when it is not in use. Behind the kitchen is the bathroom.

Storage problems in this small studio were solved by the original design of the furniture.

The bedroom is located above the kitchen and bathroom, making the living room – without a doubt the room where one spends most of the time – a larger space.

Residence in Barcelona

Two grille windows, with a metallic structure to hold the panes that make them up, bring light to the entire area of this single-environment apartment in Barcelona, with a kitchen, living area, dining area and a sleeping area (a foldaway bed occupies the space in front of the dining table). The bathroom is behind the kitchen, just opposite the entrance door. The high ceilings and the use of natural-colored wooden strips help to give a sensation of expanse to this space with an area of 300 ft^2, in which the basic rooms of a bigger home have been condensed and joined together. Facing the kitchen a storage space has been designed, enclosing the television and the refrigerator, as well as various cupboards and drawers of different sizes.

The kitchen and bedroom take up the central area of the apartment. The living room is situated near the large windows to make the most of the light.

The television, refrigerator, cupboards and storage drawers are all at the same level, with none of them jutting out, and this visually streamlines the area where they are situated.

Hakone House

Located in a small vacation resort 75 miles south-west of Tokyo, this house, built in 2002, has a rectangular floor plan measuring approximately 1,000 ft². Although it is situated in a wooded area – the house faces the mountains to the north – it is densely populated. From the outset, the aim of the project was for the home to have a good view of the surroundings and plenty of natural light. So various spaces, of different heights, have been created within a single structure which receive natural light and views of the surroundings. The large picture windows exploit the natural light available to the maximum, but without opening the home fully to the outside, which helps to preserve the privacy of the owners, who have the sensation of living in the middle of nature and not in a densely populated area. The light-colored timber flooring creates a relaxed, natural, almost Zen-like atmosphere.

The choice of modern and minimalist furniture reinforces the Zen atmosphere of the home's interior.

The plot that the house stands on is not entirely flat, so a slight slope has to be dealt with. This has been done by building a small metal staircase with five steps giving access to the inside of the home.

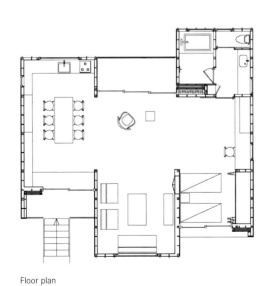

Floor plan

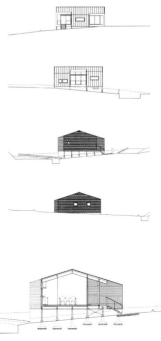

Sections

Photos: © Simone Rosberg

Apartment in Berlin

What is the most original way to divide the space in this Berlin apartment into three or four areas while preserving the atmosphere of a loft? The solution is to create two irregularly-shaped rooms in the center of the apartment. These "two rooms in one" house the bathroom and a storage area and, as well as being two separate rooms, they also act as "walls" dividing the loft into four separate areas: dining room, living room, kitchen and bedroom. A curtain hanging from a rail attached to the ceiling divides the dining-living room into two separate rooms, or it can be drawn back to create a single space. The irregular shapes of the two central structures provide the apartment with energy and represent a daring, non-orthodox alternative to the predictable division into square or rectangular rooms.

Simple furniture and the contrast of colors are other elements that define this unique loft.

Although the color of the walls in the two central spaces is not exactly the same as that of the ceiling, it is the mahogany wall at the end that breaks the monotonous color scheme of the whole.

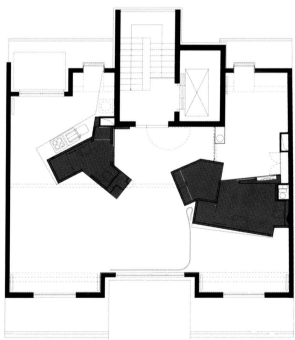

Floor plan

Home in New York

This apartment is the result of joining two symmetrical but separate studios that occupied the same floor of the building. The current owner had been renting one of the studios for some time when its owners put it up for sale. Soon afterwards, the adjacent studio was put up for sale and the tenant bought both apartments for a good price, which was something unusual in busy Manhattan. The problem lay in joining them together and hiding the architectural scar resulting from their separation. The wall separating the two apartments was knocked down and one of the load-bearing beams was hidden by the false ceiling. New timber flooring was laid to give visual unity to the two spaces. Four windows enable natural light to flood the kitchen, dining room and living room. The bedroom is behind a cupboard that doubles as a partition and has sliding etched glass panels. The bathroom, next to the bedroom, has a jacuzzi and a stainless steel hand basin.

The wardrobes facing the bed form a wall which separates the living room from the bedroom, providing the latter with privacy.

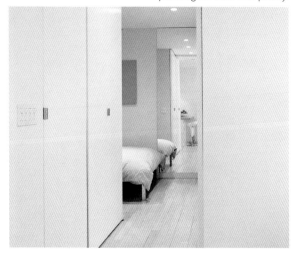

A stainless steel bar, five feet long, separates the kitchen from the dining room without blocking the light coming through the windows. Two stools enable the bar to be used as an informal dining table.

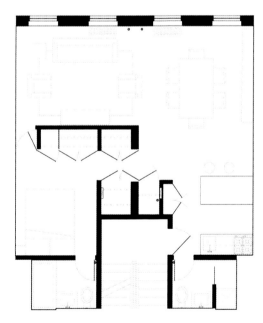

Floor plan

Loft in Milan

Kitchen, bathroom, shower room, bedroom, living room and even a chimney piece, all gently squeezed into an area of just 170 ft². The refurbishment of this studio in Milan has kept the original timber beams and divided the space into three different areas: a strip five feet wide along one of the studio's two shorter walls contains the kitchen, shower room and clothes closet, while a symmetrical strip along the other wall has the chimney piece and the bathroom. The central space, the "apartment" itself, has a double sofa bed and a dining table. Two windows light up the space and provide through ventilation. The white walls and the light timber floor and small slats make the space look bigger and make the most of the light.

The study of the space has resulted in a precise and rational distribution.

The red sofa bed lends color to a space which, because of its small size, needs to avoid being cluttered up with too many decorative details.

Floor plan

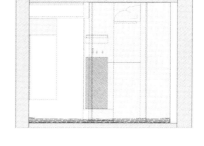

Section

Photos: © Jordi Miralles

Waxter Apartment

The only request that the owner of this New York apartment made to the architects in charge of the refurbishment was to create a functional, smart and attractive space for an art dealer, where the works of art he owned would stand out. So it was decided to use bright neutral colors, which would enable the works to shine through the purely functional elements of the decor. The various areas of the apartment (kitchen, bathroom, dining room and bedroom) are clearly defined while being flexible at the same time, enabling them to be changed at will by simply moving some of the furniture. The result is a compact, highly organized space, in which storage room has been exploited to the full, and almost all the decorative and functional features, such as light switches, have been designed and installed to save space.

The cupboard doors in the kitchen are opaque and transparent, thus breaking the monotony.

In order to exploit the light coming in through the small window to the right of the kitchen, cupboards have been installed at a 60° angle to the kitchen, enabling the light to reflect off their glass doors and spread throughout the room.

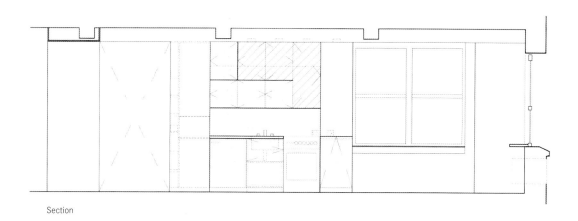

Section

Valnastine/Shein Loft

A spectacular, thick, exposed adobe brick wall is the central feature of this New York apartment. Two arched doorways in the wall connect the dining room and living room with the master bedroom and the children's room. The contrast between the dark timber flooring and the brick wall upstages the calculated minimalism of the kitchen, which has a stainless steel bar supported on a couple of metal legs. A wooden table separates the kitchen area from the living room. As many cupboards as space allowed have been installed all round the edge of the kitchen, in an effort to free up the transit areas of the apartment. The high ceilings visually alleviate the mass of the brick wall, a feature that tends to upstage all the other decorative elements in the home.

The modern and minimalist decoration creates an important contrast with the big brick wall.

The photo clearly shows the arch, the curved structure crowning one of the doorways in the brick wall, as well as the jamb, the vertical part of the door frame. The wall is thick enough to insulate the two spaces either side of it.

Photos: © Carlos Domínguez

Home in London

The visual linking of all the spaces in this apartment was the main objective of the architects commissioned for this project. This is why a handrail was installed on the upper floor with the banisters replaced by translucent panels that allow the light through but preserve privacy. A double swing door connects the living room with the hall where there are stairs leading to the upper floor. The highest point in the ceiling has been used to gain a second floor for the apartment. The roomy, well-lit kitchen also opens onto the rest of the spaces in the house by means of a bar. On top of this is a metal sheet, similar to a pull-down blind, which enables the kitchen to be masked when not in use. Timber and aluminum are the materials that have mostly been used in the kitchen. The timber provides warmth and a relaxed atmosphere, while aluminum makes the kitchen an aesthetically modern and functional room.

The bathrooms also have modern and functional aesthetics and a warm atmosphere.

The venetian blind in the kitchen regulates the light coming in through the window. The fitting under the window has had to be adapted to the slight slope in the wall.

Studio in Barcelona

Not much space is needed to have two completely different ambiences in one room. In this small apartment in Barcelona, the main room has been divided into a living area and a kitchen-diner. The first environment is defined by a two-seater sofa. The second houses the kitchen, the refrigerator – situated by space constraints against the opposite wall – and the dining table, lit by two windows. The apartment's original timber beams have been kept, stripped and painted white, as have the ceiling and the walls. The partition separating the bedroom from the main area of the home contains the shower room and bathroom, thereby exploiting space which would normally be unused. The bathroom has been tiled with 1 x 1 inch tesserae and is lit by a wall lamp similar to a light box, installed on the wall facing the shower rail.

Unique pieces of furniture, such as the table and chairs or the fridge, add a touch of character to the room.

The partition housing the shower room and bathroom has been painted in a dark color to clearly distinguish it from the adjoining stone wall, in a powerful contrast that creates an interesting visual effect. On this dark background the refrigerator stands out as a further decorative feature.

La Magdalena

In this apartment in Bogotá the central space has been divided into two separate areas: the living room, arranged round a fireplace, and the bedroom masked by a partition that is just a little bit wider than the double bed. The attention is drawn by the unusual decor in the kitchen, cluttered and almost baroque. Materials, colors and purely decorative features have been combined to create an atmosphere that is at once traditional and modern. This is shown by the contrast between the red of the walls and the ceiling moldings, and the black of the wall tiles, or the counterpoint created by the wooden shelves and cabinets and the chrome hooks for the pots and pans. The bathroom is also a mixture of styles, with a marble handbasin and a retro-inspired faucet, contrasting with copper-colored piping acting as an ornamental feature.

All kitchen utensils are on view. Their layout creates a unique decoration and atmosphere.

Small niches have been opened up in the two walls leading to the kitchen which act as shelves for decorative elements. The rough finish of the wall is another of the discordant features that are to be found in the kitchen and which provide the space with character.

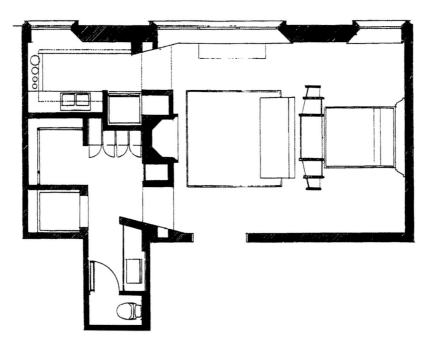

Floor plan

Home in Shepherd's Bush

A closet housing a work table and plenty of storage space are just some of the numerous decorative and functional details implemented in this London home in order to save as much space as possible. The wooden floor links the various spaces in the apartment, in which all unnecessary partitions or dividing features which might block circulation or the light have been removed. The kitchen has a small bar which doubles as a dining table for informal meals and facing it are two stools. The well-lit home also has a built-in false chimney piece which the owners use as a shelf for various decorative elements.

The renovation of the small apartment has created ample, cozy and well-lit spaces.

The clever lay-out of the bedroom enables the desk, which rests on a trestle when it is unfolded, to receive plenty of natural light.

Studio in Sydney

There are two features that stand out in this Sydney apartment, situated in the heart of Kings Cross, which before its refurbishment was a cramped and impractical studio: a sliding wall, a work of art by Tim Richardson, and a long, red-lacquered closet running right through the apartment which houses practically all the home's utilities, from the hi-fi to the kitchen hob. This spectacular piece has been built to look like a Swiss army knife; hence its striking color which is also a nod to Sydney's red light district where the apartment is situated. The contrast between Tim Richardson's work of art and the closet, which has become the backbone of the home and creates a clear distinction between the old and the new, gives the home an unusual avant-garde character. The result is a space that is dynamic and relaxing at the same time, with a marked avant-garde atmosphere.

The sliding wall separates the bedroom from the living room. When closed it breaks the continuity of the red piece of furniture.

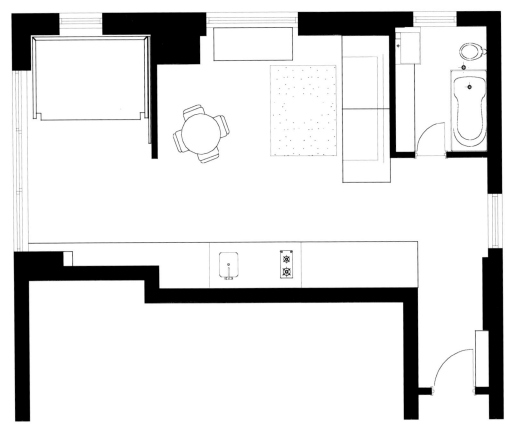

Floor plan

The closet, which among other features houses the cooker, runs down the wall from one end of the apartment to the other. Facing it are the bedroom, living room and bathroom.

MP3 Residence

This apartment was refurbished by juggling with the concepts of visibility and privacy. A series of glass panels separate the various areas and levels in the home. One of these panels splits up the dining room and the kitchen and serves as a support for the one-legged dining table. Another panel, rising right up to the roof, separates the two sections of the staircase that connects the two (and a half) levels in the home, and yet another has been used as a wall for the studio, situated half a level above the upper floor. This also houses the bedroom and a living room. The glass allows the light to go through the apartment from end to end, and breaks with any pre-conceived notions about the concepts of intimacy and privacy. Two works of art by the artist Stephan Brugerman complete this avant-garde design: a piece called No Program, which reproduces the colored bars seen at the end of television transmission, and the text "This is not supposed to be here", printed on one of the walls.

The bedroom has a sofa, center table and television, which turns on an axle so that it can be seen from the bed.

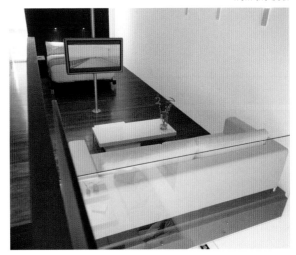

Half a level below the entrance hall we find one of the house's two living rooms; further back are the dining room, the kitchen and the stairs leading to the second floor.

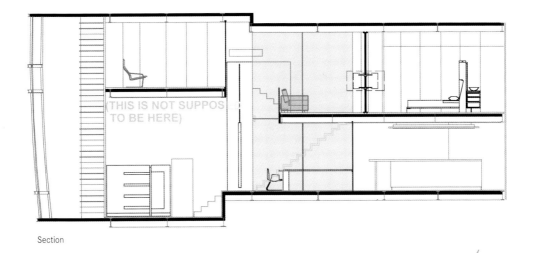

Section

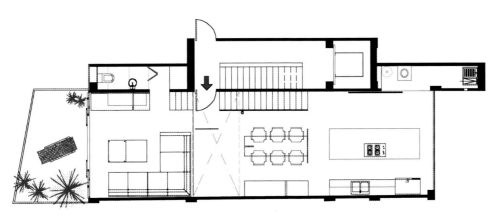

Ground floor

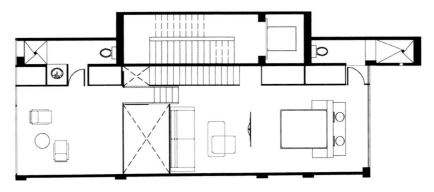

First floor

Apartment in Turin

Nowadays glass is one of the materials that is most used in small apartments or those that have poor natural light. Its advantages are obvious: from a purely practical standpoint, glass helps to lighten the space by connecting the various areas of the home and enabling light to penetrate without any obstacles. Aesthetically, it breaks up the feeling of isolation caused by opaque walls, whatever the material, and give the home a relaxed atmosphere in which the traditional boundaries between private and public space are removed. This is the case with this apartment, in which the glass has been used to visually connect the two floors as well as to enable the light to reach every corner. A shelf unit going right up to the ceiling beams and embedded in them exploits the limited storage space to the full. Unlike the usual arrangement in duplexes, the kitchen is on the upper floor.

Excellent finishes and subtle decoration create an elegant and functional apartment.

An attic window lights up the upper floor. The landing and the upper section of stairs are of glass, enabling the light to reach the ground floor as well. In this respect, the landing acts as a skylight sending light straight down on to the space beneath.

Photos: © Margherita Spiluttini

Studio in Vienna

Two features stand out in this studio in Vienna. Firstly, the large sun-blind-type window that fully opens the home to the outside. When it is open, this window turns the space below it into a balcony; or when it is shut, it keeps it as a gallery. Secondly, the architects' unusual fondness for irregular structures: sloping walls, diagonally-laid beams, platforms, furniture that follows the irregular line of the walls, and so on. The result is an unusual apartment in which the lack of space is made up for by the original shaping applied. A skylight and a window jutting out from the facade light up the bathroom, while the combination of materials (timber, aluminum and glass) give the space an avant-garde atmosphere.

The dividing wall between the entrance and the bath area is used to install a cupboard.

The window lighting up the bathroom juts out from the metal facade, an added feature of the building, while the sun-blind-type window provides an original balcony.

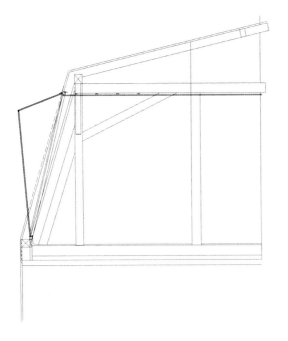

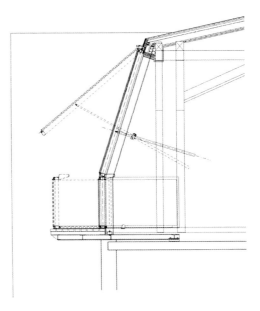

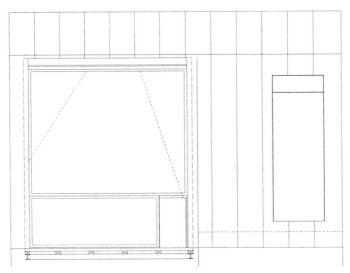

Constructive details

May Loft

Lakonis Architekten were commissioned to transform a medium-sized, well-lit apartment, but divided into several narrow rooms, into an open-plan, fluid space. To do this, they knocked down practically all the existing partitions in the original apartment and divided it into two completely distinct areas: the main space housing the living room and dining room, and another where the utility areas have been concentrated (kitchen, bathroom and bedroom). Various niches have been built into the walls surrounding the bathroom for keeping books, clothes or decorative items. It was decided to install a module in the kitchen to house the hob as well as the oven, the dishwasher and the sink, so that one could easily walk round it. Five windows light up the dining/sitting room, whose expanse provides two separate atmospheres.

The color red in the bedroom and in the kitchen adds character to the apartment and breaks with the predominant color white.

A large room with different atmospheres
was created by knocking down the partition
walls separating the apartment's rooms.
The chosen furniture, with contemporary
lines, emphasizes the spaciousness and
luminosity of the room.

Apartment in Barcelona

An elongated space poses problems when deciding on the room distribution. In this Barcelona apartment, the problem has been resolved by putting the bedrooms and the bathroom in the central zone and keeping the two ends of the home, which receive the most light, for the living room and kitchen. Facing the latter is the dining table, converted into an extension of the sink. The living room is at the same level as the outside landing, while the rest of the house has been raised a few inches higher. The difference in level is overcome by a wooden step in the doorway connecting the living room with the rest of the house. To make up for the lack of natural light, ceiling spotlights have been installed right through the house, while practically half the surface of the side walls in the bedrooms is of translucent glass, which lets the light through but prevents one seeing clearly behind it.

The clear colors of the walls and floor create an atmosphere of neutral tones which contribute to good illumination.

The apartment has good through ventilation via its central passage, but its excessive length prevents the light coming from the two ends from reaching the central space. Therefore there was not much point in knocking down the bedroom walls to gain more light.

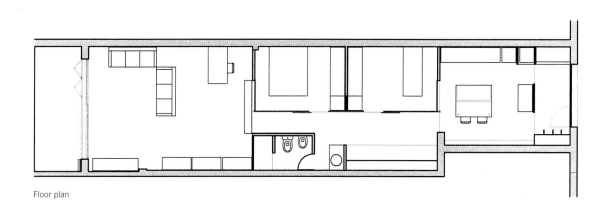

Floor plan

Cocoon House

Two hours by road from Melbourne, in steep mountainous surroundings, is the spectacular Cocoon House. This oval house, shaped like an American football, rests on metal columns and is a clever and eminently practical response to the frequently cold and windy climate and ground conditions of the plot it stands on. The house, whose aerodynamic shapes minimizes wind resistance, rests on metal feet on a pronounced slope. To resolve the difference in levels, a metal walkway with timber decking connects the house with the plot. The interior has been structured as if it were a caravan: the bedroom is at one end, the "tip" of the oval, while the bathroom occupies a narrow central strip in the home. The rest of the structure has been given over to the dining/living room, with an open plan kitchen, a timber bar and a small balcony affording views of the leafy forest surrounding the house.

Cocoon house emerges from leafy surroundings full of trees as if it were a supernatural object.

The exterior structure, built with parallel
metal sheets that come together at the
ends, gives it an unusual industrial look,
as if it were a modern Zeppelin.

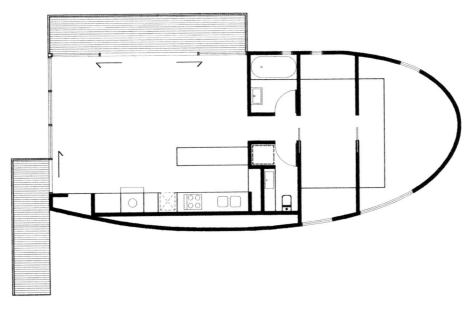

Floor plan

Wee Residence

This is a structure with a square floor plan, situated in an area with extreme winter temperatures, standing on the ground and some small metal columns, thereby compensating for a slight difference in level. The exterior is of rusted steel, while all the interior surfaces (walls, ceilings and flooring) are of fir wood, which helps to integrate the house into its surroundings. The home has a prefabricated fireplace and opens fully to the exterior by means of two sliding glass panel walls. At one end of the home are the two beds – at different heights, as if they were bunks, to make better use of the space – two storage chests, a closet and a chest of drawers. At the other end are the kitchen, several oak shelving units and the dining table. A pair of armchairs completes the furnishing of a home that willingly takes a back seat to the beautiful landscape on view from inside.

The reduced dimensions and basic furniture make this home the perfect retreat for weekends or holidays.

The fir wood used on the exterior and the oak used inside provide the home with warmth and blend it seamlessly into a practically unspoiled landscape.

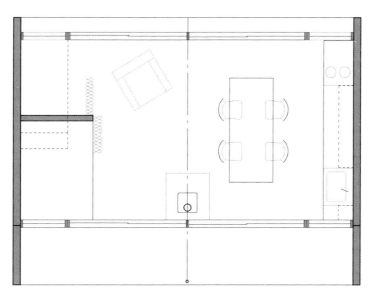

Floor plan

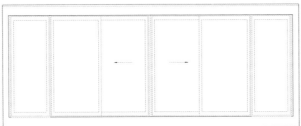

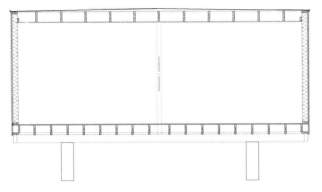

Sections

Boathouse

Built on a floating timber platform, this home contains all the comforts of a more spacious, traditional house on dry land. Timber is the predominant material used in the construction. Most of the exterior wall round the house have been replaced by sliding wooden doors with glass mullions, affording views of the surroundings. A strip five feet wide runs round the house as if it were a balcony, and separates it from the handrail, which has tautened metal cables between each banister. Inside there are two double bedrooms and a living/dining room with integrated kitchen. Drawers and storage shelves have been built under the beds, while for the lighting there are wedge-shaped wooden wall lights that integrate into the decor of the home. A flat roof, with built-in spotlights to light up the perimeter strip, covers the house.

Adapted to its means, this construction allows for a different and original way of life.

All the essential appliances and
accessories have been installed in the
kitchen: refrigerator, microwave oven,
television, sink and oven. The work-top
is of stainless steel.

Keenan Tower

The Keenan Tower, situated in Old Wire Road in Fayetteville, is an eighty-foot-high structure, similar to a forest ranger's observation tower. Owned by Stacy and James Keenan and designed by the architect, Marlon Blackwell, the tower has been built with oak and steel. The structure consists of a steel skeleton, clad in sheets of white oak which let in the light. The house towers over the surrounding treetops and boasts simply amazing 360° views. Designed in terms of the changes in light caused by the path of the sun, the house has varying atmospheres depending on the time of day. The Keenan Tower has been designed as a look-out point, which is why the wall of the main level is an enormous picture window. Above the main level, we come across the real look-out point, open to the sky, which doubles as a dining area. A kitchen, bathroom and storage area complete the home.

This unique project perfectly fits in with the wooded landscape of this city in the state of Arkansas.

The open-air look-out point on the upper floor is used by the owners as a dining area. A blind controls the amount of light coming in at this level through the window, while on one of the sides we find a small balcony that doubles as an individual look-out point, and on the other side, a window.

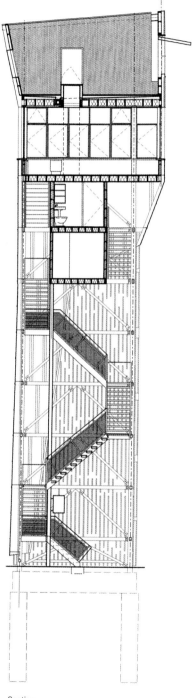

Section

M & R House

The first thing that strikes one about the M & R House is its unusual structure, formed by three dissimilar blocks joined together, and its striking green color, which integrates it into its natural surroundings. The three blocks or cubes that make it up are situated on a slightly sloping plot, and this is why the architects designed each level as a "step" in a staircase. In fact, a metal staircase connects the three structures, two of which (the top two) are twice as high. The kitchen, the central space in the home, has been situated in the middle block, for which the roof of the lower block doubles as a patio. The exterior walls are made up of panels in different shades of green, thereby establishing an unusual dialog between the surrounding vegetation and the house.

The industrial aesthetic of the house's interior creates a contrast with the mountainous landscape of the exterior.

Large windows enable full advantage to be taken of the abundant natural light entering the house and, at the same time, remove the traditional separation between inside and outside.

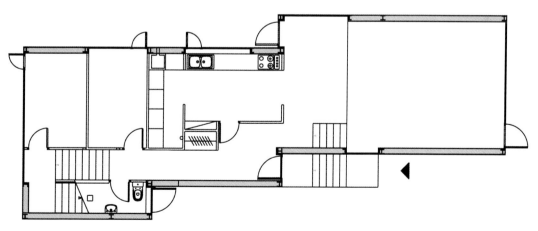

Floor plan

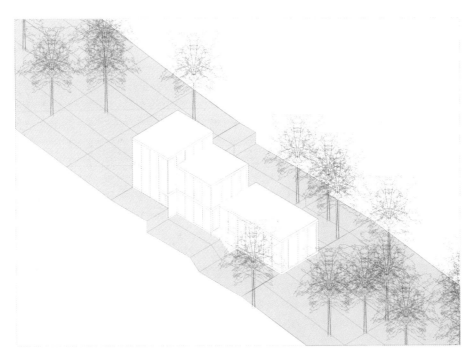

Axonometric view

Perspective

Duplex in Stockholm

Minimalism and visual lightness were two basic principles for the designers of this project, a duplex in Stockholm. The influence of Scandinavian design and minimalism can be seen throughout the home, a clear example of what can be achieved in a restricted area thanks to the clever use of materials and an ingenious lay-out. The staircase connecting the two levels consists of steps joined to the wall, without any integrating structure, leaving the space visually uncluttered while introducing an interesting set of pure lines that offset the functional and straight-edged furnishings. Starkness and moderation, also to be found in the pictures, govern the decor of this apartment, in there are hardly any curved forms. On the lower level, with its light timber flooring, are the dining/living room, kitchen and bathroom, and on the upper level the work area and the bedroom. A small patio completes the lay-out of the apartment.

Despite the minimalism of the furniture and the straight lines, the duplex's interior does not lack warmth or comfort.

The few carefully-chosen decorative details, as well as the furniture, stand out for their coldness. However, the result gains warmth thanks to the materials that they are made of, mainly different types of wood.

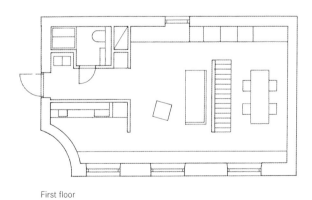

First floor

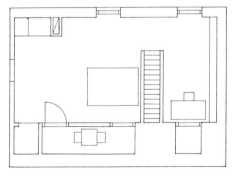

Second floor

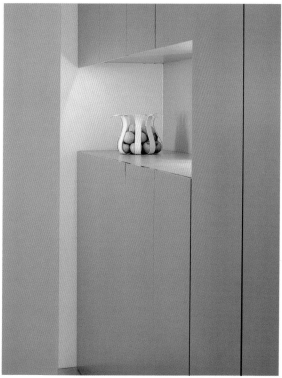

Studio in London

In this small London apartment, a second level has been gained by taking advantage of the attic situated over the kitchen. The attic, reached by an original steep staircase, has been fitted out as a relaxation zone, but it can also be used as a guest room. On the lower level is the dining/living room, the (open-plan) kitchen, the bedrooms and the bathroom which is masked by a red sliding panel. The staircase, framing the right-hand side of the kitchen, has irregularly-shaped hollow steps, which makes it useful for holding certain kitchen utensils. The apartment is in the top floor of the building, so the ceiling has the shape of the gabled roof. The wooden kitchen floor and fittings bring warmth to the apartment, which has red decorative features scattered around it (the panel separating the bathroom from the bedroom, the false fireplace, the chairs and armchair in the dining room, and so on).

Some elements, such as the use of wood and an original staircase, give the studio a particular character.

Four built-in halogen lamps in the ceiling (which is also the floor of the attic) light up the bathroom area, while various wall lamps do the same job in the dining/living room. A window floods the bedroom with natural light.

Photos: © Carlos Domínguez

Apartment in London

White and shades of cream have been chosen as unifying elements for the various spaces in this apartment. The light color of the ceiling, floor, walls and even the furnishings means that full advantage is taken of the natural light and makes the space look bigger. The dining/living room is the central area of the house. The sliding glass panels in the living room lead to the kitchen and bedroom, which has a private bathroom. The built-in closets save space and are content to be upstaged by the rest of the furniture, such as the bed, armchair and bedside table in the bedroom. The kitchen introduces a note of color with its turquoise work top, which reflects the light from the spotlights built into the overhead cabinets. The dining area has been divided into two completely different atmospheres: the living area, arranged round a low coffee table, and the dining area, where the leading role is played by the table, also of glass, occupying the center.

The subdued and elegant decoration helps create an ethereal and bright atmosphere.

Glass doors are lighter than those made of any other material (whether it be wood, metal or plastic). For this reason, they are the most advisable for lightening up the space.

Denise Lee Home

Having a small indoor patio in a crowded city like London is a privilege that must not be wasted. In this small apartment, it has been decided to open the dining/living room to the outside by means of a glass wall with a sliding door, so that the outside can be enjoyed even indoors. Thus the natural light from the outside meets no obstacles and penetrates into every corner of the home. The wall separating the kitchen from the rest of the house has been reduced to install in its place glass blocks, which allow light to pass through and act as space dividers. The kitchen has a parallel lay-out, with one side being the work area and the opposite side housing the oven, refrigerator and various built-in cabinets. The result is an uncluttered room in which the owners can move about freely.

The furniture adds a unique touch which demonstrates a personal style and moves away from conventional decoration.

The three halogen lamps lighting up
the dining room are built into a small
organic-shaped structure that lends
an avant-garde, unconventional touch
to the home.

Loftcube

This is a prefabricated home that can be modified to the consumer's taste. The four walls of the house can be transparent, translucent or completely shut off from the outside, although it is also possible to ask for combinations of these three options. The windows have wooden strips to air the house and control the amount of light coming in. The inside of the house can also be adapted to the tastes of the owner. The house has a relaxation area, a kitchen, bathroom and living room. The area of these spaces can be changed by simply sliding the panels that can be seen in the photographs. The shower hose can be directed either side of the panel to water the plants growing in the small bed beneath it. Loftcube is designed to be installed on urban patios. The structure is transported by helicopter once the patio has been prepared to take the weight of the home. The Loftcube has an area of 430 ft2.

Designed by Studio Aisslinger, Loftcube is one of the most important proposals of mobile architecture of the last few years.

Access to the Loftcube, which is
approximately five feet above the ground,
is by a small wooden stairway. The home
has been designed as if it were an attic
on top of another attic, which is a new
way of dealing with urban space.

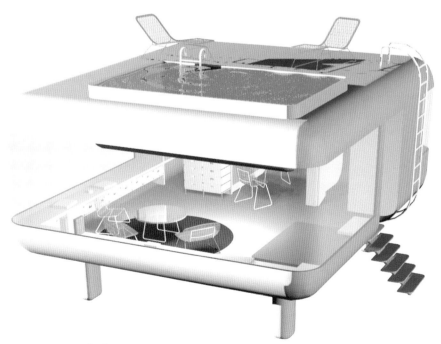

Render

Apartment in Rome

An extremely narrow apartment can be a nightmare when planning its lay-out. The problem is aggravated in the utility areas – kitchen and bathroom – which in most homes are built near each other to exploit the mains water supply. In this apartment, the problem was solved by building an oval central area integrating the bathroom and kitchen. There was even room for a small passage running through the oval from side to side, thereby doing away with the need to go right round it to get from the bedroom to the entrance (or vice versa). At each end of the apartment are the bedroom and the dining/living room. The glass block walls enable good use to be made of the natural light coming in through the four windows, while the darkwood floor unifies the two spaces at each end of the house, giving them continuity (the floor in the central oval is of light wood, setting it apart from the other spaces at first sight).

Simple and colorful furniture contrasts with the white of the oval and creates a warm and young atmosphere.

The central oval gives onto the entrance door and has a small built-in bookcase. In the kitchen the wall does not go up all the way to the ceiling, so as to allow natural light into the living room.

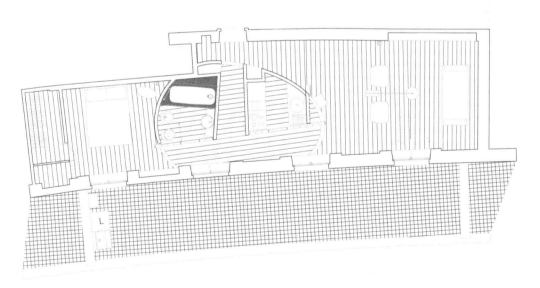

Floor plan

Floating house

This home, standing on a floating wooden platform, has been built following the aesthetic lines (portholes, bunks) as well as structural lines of a sailing vessel. The height of the ceiling has been made use of to install hanging bunks which are reached by means of a wooden ladder. The house has a compact kitchen, a small dining table, a bathroom, a work area and a living room. The outside of the home, a three-foot-wide strip that goes right round it, is big enough to place a small table and a couple of stools. The windows have roller blinds or, in a few cases, venetian blinds. The floor, inside walls and most of the furniture are of wood. The back of the house has a structure that enables a canopy to be unrolled to gain privacy inside.

Illuminated corners give other areas of the house, such as the staircase, a corner in the living room and a balcony, more importance.

Despite the almost complete predominance
of wood, both inside and outside the home,
the frames of the sliding glass doors are
metal.

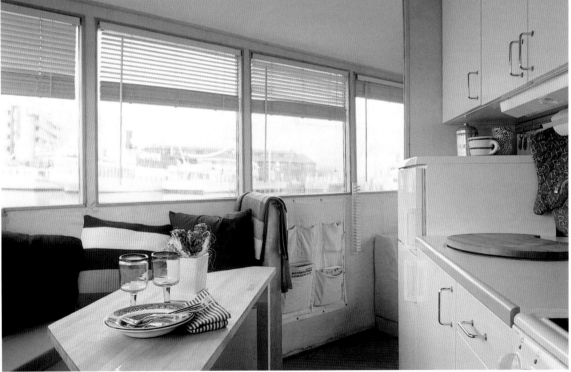

Attic in Zurich

This apartment is the result of the transformation and refurbishment of an attic in the Wüstemann house in Zurich, which has splendid views of the lake to the south, the city to the west and the nearby forest to the east. The roof became a structure with its own identity by being joined visually to the ground. The name of the home ("The Hammer") comes from the hammer-shaped structure which jutted out from the former space and whose dimensions were entirely dependent on the requirements of the design. The timber structure in the original space was kept so that its appearance would contrast with the new elements and bring a dynamic quality to the loft, while making it a reminder of the original apartment. The variety of structures between the old beams, the new ceiling, the gabled roof and the stairway produces attractive light effects in the apartment, which thereby changes its character as the sun changes its position and provides unusual nuances to the whole.

Illuminated corners give other areas of the house, such as the staircase, a corner in the living room and a balcony, more importance.

A dark floor is usually not recommended if one wants to make the most of existing natural light. However, in very well-lit homes, these floors can be a striking decorative element.

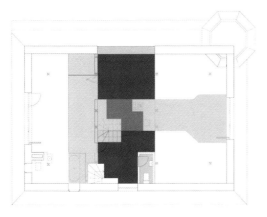

First floor

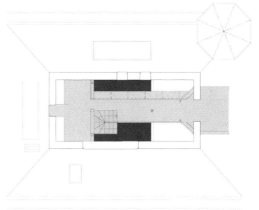

Second floor

Apartment in Castiglione

The central feature of this apartment is the wall housing the bathroom and kitchen, decorated with an enormous black and white photograph. Not only does the wall separate the utility spaces from the rest of the rooms, it is also the main decorative feature of the house. The lack of space in the kitchen has been resolved by laying out the fittings into two parallel rows and having one of them steal a bit of the bathroom space to leave a central working area free. In the central area of the home the various spaces have been defined not by walls but by means of furnishings or decorative features. The wall mirror at the end is in fact a cabinet in four modules, while the bed has been "boxed in" by a piece of furniture similar to a closet, whose function is to preserve privacy as well as act as a visual separation between the sleeping area and the rest of the areas. The piece of furniture housing the bed has various drawers and space-saving storage facilities.

A box made of composite wood, which contains the bed, is a made-to-measure mobile piece of furniture.

Most of the home's decorative features, such as the venetian blinds, the glass shelf unit and the dining room mirror, have been chosen not only for aesthetic reasons, but also to make full use of the light and lighten the visual weight of the whole.

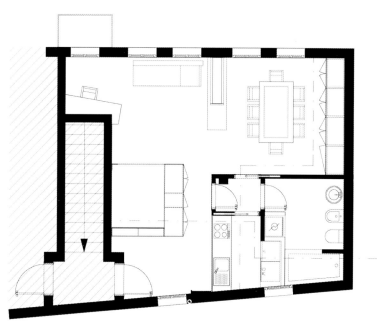

Floor plan

Photos: © Hanse Haus GmbH

Hanse Colani Rotorhouse

The design, the organic shapes and ergonomics all play their part in the setting up of a home with all conveniences within an area of just under 390 ft^2. The functional areas rotate around the disc-shaped platform on which they are to be found; hence the house's name, Rotorhouse. This rotation is not a merely aesthetic feature, but also functional, as it is space-saving and is also cheaper than building a home divided into the traditional fixed spaces. Rotorhouse is a prototype by Luigi Colani and Hanse Haus which is not yet being mass-produced, although it can be seen in the Oberleichtersbach factory. Its organic shapes do away with aggressive rectilinear shapes and drabness: blue is used for the bathroom, white for the kitchen and red for the bedroom. The exterior of the home is timber and has large windows and sliding glass doors to take full advantage of the natural light.

A futuristic interior hides behind the wooden exterior of Rotorhouse.

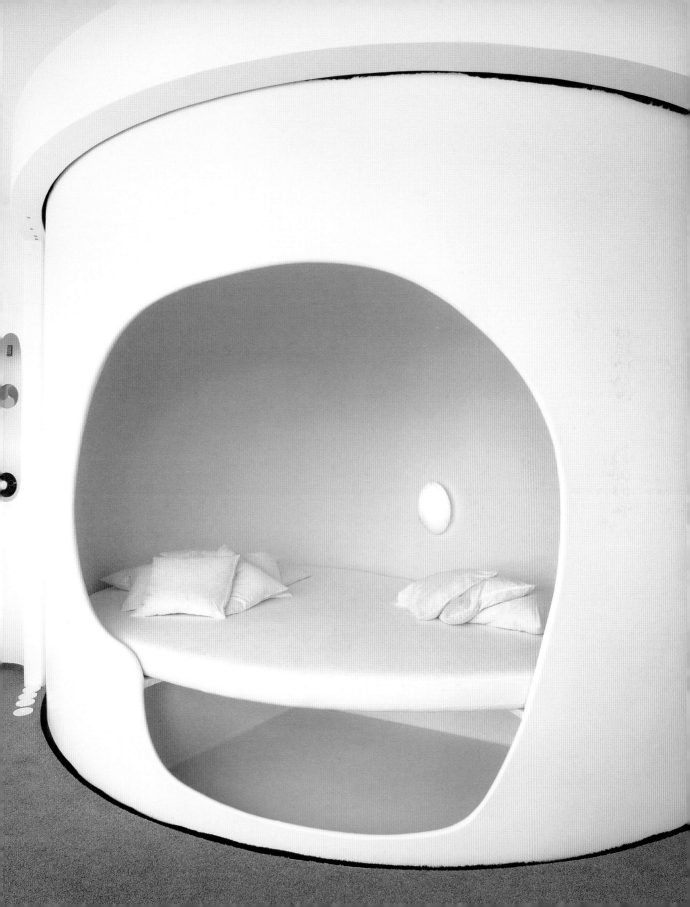

It is practically impossible to find a single right angle in the Rotorhouse, a home in which any feature considered to be "aggressive" has been excluded.

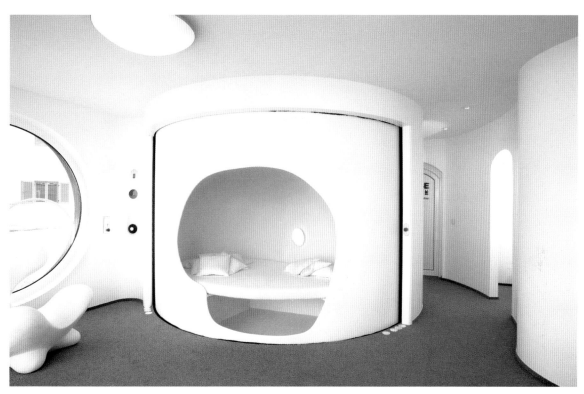

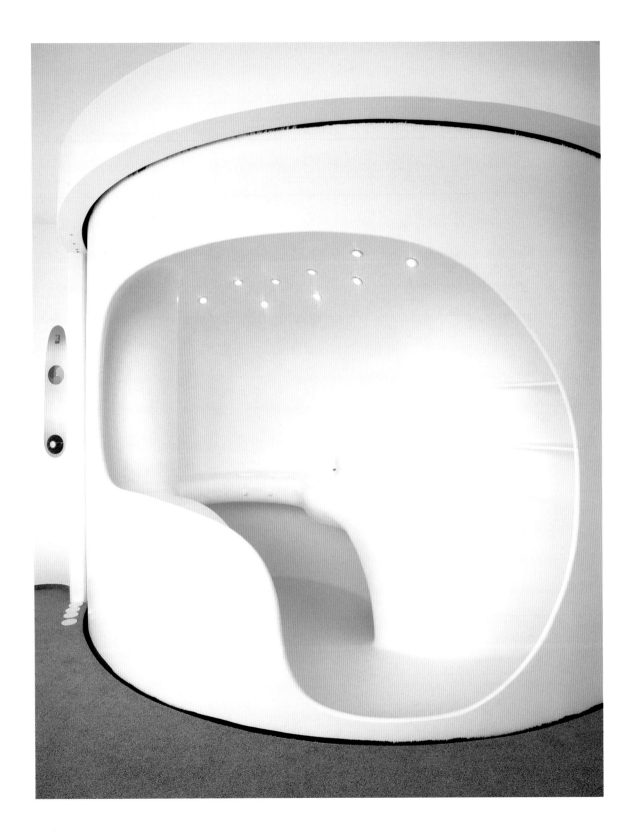

XXS House

A metal staircase with irregular steps and an almost vertical slope connects the two levels of this duplex. On the lower floor we find a space that carries out the three-fold function of dining area, living area and kitchen. The light coming in through a glass wall illuminates the space evenly and a venetian blind controls its intensity. The kitchen is very well lit by the light coming in through the window above the work top. A third source of light comes from the stairwell, from the skylights lighting up the bedroom which, situated on the upper floor, makes perfect use of its attic wall to fix the heads of the two single beds. The use of unrefined-looking material such as cement or the iron on the staircase give the home a harsh and almost industrial atmosphere, offset only by the timber flooring on the upper level.

The glass doors of the ground floor connect the house with the exterior and make the communal areas bigger.

The façade's metallic materials (also used
on the inside) give the apartment an
industrial and vanguard look.

Mich Maroney Residence

Elongated spaces are particularly difficult to work with, and more so if they are of restricted size. This is the case with this two-story London home, in which one of the two rooms on the lower floor has been turned into a living room that shares space with a four-module bookcase and a work area occupying the space under the stairs. In the adjoining room are the kitchen and the dining table. The fact that the two rooms have natural light reduces the sensation of baroque clutter caused by the crowding of features in one space. On the upper floor is the bedroom, whose main feature is a double bed facing the two windows that flood the room with light. The white of the walls and most of the furnishings (including the fabrics chosen by the owners) helps to make the space look lighter.

A cozy interior is created by making the most of natural light and carefully choosing the furniture.

● ● ● The straight wooden staircase, with banisters going up to the ceiling, leading to the upper floor, has its right-hand side flush to the wall, leaving a space that is occupied by the work table.

Unit P-18A

The main problems facing the architects John Friedman and Alice Kimm when renovating this Upper East Side apartment were the unusual ceiling height and the fact that, as a result, the tiny rooms that the space had been divided into seemed even smaller than they actually were. The aim, which was to convert the space into a well-lit open-plan apartment, in which the various rooms would seamlessly relate to each other, was achieved by getting rid of most of the existing partitions and building a false ceiling to lower the height of the actual ceiling over most of its area, which was then split in certain places, abutting at right angles with the partitions separating, for example, the kitchen from the living and dining area. The contrast of materials and the use of an array of colors, a solution barely employed in the original apartment, completed a spectacular refurbishment.

The opening-up of the kitchen wall increases the structural dynamics created by the partition wall and false ceilings.

The white of the walls enables the natural light to be exploited to the full, while functioning as a backdrop that visually highlights any piece of furniture or decorative feature.